CLASSICAL

Frédéric
CHOPIN

by Joanne Mattern
with Consultation by John Viscardi,
Executive Director of Classic Lyric Arts
illustrated by Marilena Perilli

RED CHAIR PRESS

Egremont, Massachusetts

Classical Composers has been produced and published by Red Chair Press Books for Young Readers:
Red Chair Press LLC   PO Box 333   South Egremont, MA 01258
www.redchairpress.com

 Download a Free Activity Guide on our website.

For more information about Classic Lyric Arts, visit www.classiclyricarts.org.

Names: Mattern, Joanne, 1963- author. | Viscardi, John, consultant. | Perilli, Marilena, illustrator.

Title: Frédéric Chopin / by Joanne Mattern, with consultation by John Viscardi, executive director of Classic Lyric Arts ; illustrated by Marilena Perilli.

Description: Egremont, Massachusetts : Red Chair Press, [2025] | Series: Classical composers | Interest age level: 007-010. | Includes bibliographical references and index. | Summary: Frédéric Chopin (1810–1849), a Polish-French composer and pianist of the Romantic era ... Colorful illustrations plus photographs of meaningful sites and settings connect readers to important points in Chopin's history. A timeline and B Sharp sidebars add details to the composer's life story.--Publisher.

Identifiers: ISBN: 978-1-64371-430-1 (LB hardcover) | 978-1-64371-431-8 (paperback) | 978-1-64371-433-2 (S&L ebook) | LCCN: 2024936081

Subjects: LCSH: Chopin, Frédéric, 1810-1849--Juvenile literature. | Composers--Poland--Biography-- Juvenile literature. | CYAC: Chopin, Frédéric, 1810-1849. | Composers--Poland--Biography. | LCGFT: Biographies. | BISAC: JUVENILE NONFICTION / Biography & Autobiography / Music. | JUVENILE NONFICTION / Biography & Autobiography / Performing Arts. | JUVENILE NONFICTION / Music / Classical.

Classification: LCC: ML410.C54 M38 2025 | DDC: 780.92--dc23

Copyright © 2026 Red Chair Press LLC
RED CHAIR PRESS, the RED CHAIR and associated logos are
registered trademarks of Red Chair Press LLC.

All rights reserved. No part of this book may be reproduced, stored in an information or retrieval system, or transmitted in any form by any means, electronic, mechanical including photocopying, recording, or otherwise without the prior written permission from the Publisher. For permissions, contact info@redchairpress.com

Image credits: Cover, pp. 4, 12, 15, 16-17, 28, 29, 31 ©Shutterstock; p. 13 © Photo © Berko Fine Paintings, Knokke-Heist, Belgium/Bridgeman Images; p. 22 © Look and Learn/Elgar Collection / Bridgeman Images; p. 28 © GL Archive/Alamy.

Illustrations: Marilena Perilli, except p. 7 by Joe LeMonnier

Printed in the United States of America

0425 1P CGF25

Table of Contents

A Talented Child 4
Leaving Poland 12
Frédéric Chopin, Superstar! 22
An Amazing Talent 28
Timeline 30
Glossary 32
Read More 32
Index 32

A Talented Child

Frédéric Chopin (FREH-duh-rik show-PAN) was one of the world's greatest composers. He wrote beautiful music for the piano. He is called Poland's most famous composer.

Frédéric was born in a little town near Warsaw, Poland, on March 1, 1810. His father, Nicholas, had moved to Poland, the Duchy of Warsaw, from France. He worked as a **tutor** for rich families.

Frédéric's mother was Polish. Her name was Justyna. Justyna loved music. She made sure her children had piano lessons when they were very young. When Frédéric was a child, he used to lie under the piano while his older sister played. That way he could hear and "feel" the music.

Europe in 1810

Once Frédéric began playing the piano, his parents realized he was quite talented. When Frédéric was six years old, they hired Wojciech (VOY-cheh) Zywny to teach him.

Zywny was a good teacher. He did not just teach Frédéric how to play. He also taught him about great composers like Bach and Mozart. Young Frédéric loved music more than anything!

Chopin was born 60 years after Johann Sebastian Bach's death. Bach's music continued to be very popular during Chopin's life.

Wolfgang Amadaeus Mozart had been dead only 19 years when Chopin was born. His music was so popular that it would have been heard in opera houses and great halls around Europe during Chopin's lifetime.

It did not take long before Frédéric could play the piano better than his teacher. When he was only eight years old, he began performing in **salons**. The audiences could not believe how well the little boy played. They were even more surprised when they found out little Frédéric wrote his own music!

B# B SHARP: Young Frédéric also liked to have fun. He drew funny cartoons and loved to ride horses with his friends.

Leaving Poland

Later, Chopin studied with a teacher named Jozef Elsner. When Chopin was 17, he wrote a piece he titled *Variations, Opus 2*. This piece was a **variation** on music written by Mozart. As musicians began playing the new *Opus 2*, people all around Europe heard Chopin's music. They loved it!

Chopin playing the piano in Prince Radziwill's Salon, 1828. Prince Radziwill of Poland and Lithuania was one of the richest men in Europe.

Chopin was happy in Poland. But music was not as popular in Warsaw as it was in other places, such as Vienna or Paris. Also, Poland was having a lot of problems. Other countries wanted to control Poland. Poland's neighbor, Russia, even took over part of Poland's land three different times during the late 1790s.

B# **B SHARP:** When he heard Chopin's music, a famous composer Robert Schumann wrote, "Hats off! A genius!"

Chopin's birthplace and childhood home near Warsaw is now a museum.

The Musikverein, a beautiful concert hall in Vienna, Austria, was first opened in January 1870.

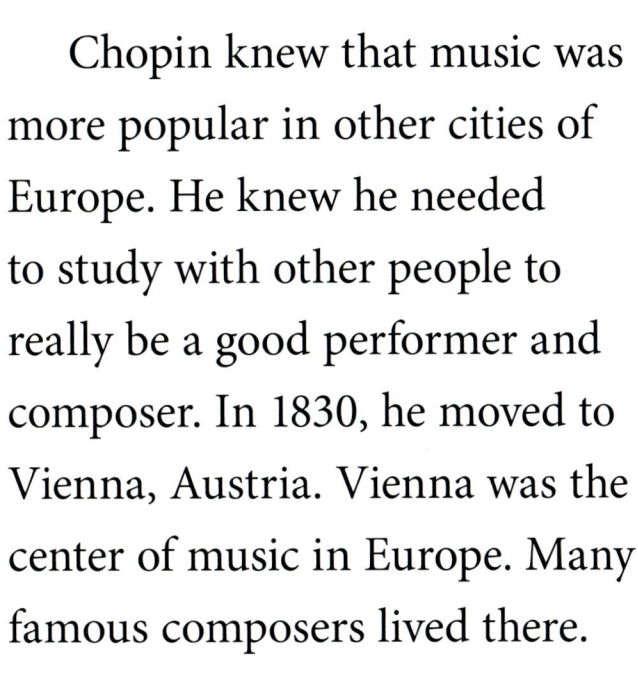

Chopin knew that music was more popular in other cities of Europe. He knew he needed to study with other people to really be a good performer and composer. In 1830, he moved to Vienna, Austria. Vienna was the center of music in Europe. Many famous composers lived there.

People in Vienna loved to watch and hear Chopin perform. His music made people feel excited and happy. Chopin's music was part of the **Romantic** period. The Romantic period started around 1830 and ended around 1900, as compositions became increasingly expressive and dramatic. Grand symphonies, big dramatic operas, and passionate songs were influenced by art and literature.

One of Chopin's favorite kinds of music was the **mazurka**. When he was growing up, Chopin often heard mazurkas. He went on to write more than 50 mazurkas. His *Mazurka in B-flat Major, Opus 7,* Number 1, is one of his most popular pieces.

Chopin preferred writing music. He had stage fright and did not like playing in front of large groups of people.

Chopin also wrote many waltzes. These were popular ballroom dances in high society. From 1829 until 1847 he wrote 14 well-loved waltzes.

Frédéric Chopin, Superstar!

Chopin only stayed in Vienna for eight months. He traveled to other countries. He played in many different concert halls.

In 1831, Chopin moved to Paris, France. He became one of the most popular musicians in Paris. He also earned money as a piano teacher. It would be much like having Beyonce as your voice coach today.

B# B SHARP: Chopin was shy about playing big concerts. He liked playing at friends' homes or at small salons better.

Chopin had a good life in Paris. He earned a lot of money. He fell in love with a woman named Aurore Dudevant. Dudevant wrote novels under the name George Sand. Chopin's new girlfriend helped him gain confidence to perform in front of larger groups of people.

Chopin performed a few concerts in Paris. But he was more interested in composing. He wrote beautiful music. Many of the pieces he wrote in Paris are considered **masterpieces** today.

B♯ B SHARP: Chopin had many musical friends in Paris. His friends included Felix Mendelssohn (FEE-lix MEN-dul-sun) and Franz Liszt (FRANZ LIST) who introduced Chopin to Ms Dudevant.

Chopin continued to write new music even when he was very sick.

In 1839, Chopin got very sick. He had an illness called **tuberculosis**. Even though he was sick, Chopin kept on writing music. One of his most famous pieces is called the "Minute Waltz." It is a short, lively piece that people love today, 180 years after it was written.

In 1847, Chopin toured England and Scotland. The tour was long and difficult. Chopin's health failed. He made his last public appearance in November 1848. Then he went home to Paris.

An Amazing Talent

Frédéric Chopin died on October 17, 1849. He was only 39 years old.

Even though he died young, Chopin is very famous. He was the first great composer who wrote just for the piano. Students and orchestras often perform his work today. And audiences love to hear Chopin's music today.

B# **B SHARP:** Chopin's body was buried in Paris. But his heart was buried in Warsaw, Poland.

Chopin's grave in Paris.

Important Dates in Frédéric Chopin's Life

1810   Frédéric Chopin is born near Warsaw, Poland.

1816   Chopin begins taking piano lessons.

1818   Chopin gives his first public concert.

1830   Chopin moves to Vienna, Austria.

1831   Chopin moves to Paris, France.

1839   Chopin becomes ill with tuberculosis.

1847   Chopin tours England and Scotland.

1849   Chopin dies on October 17 at home in Paris.

This beautiful statue is a monument to Chopin in Warsaw, Poland.

Glossary

composer a person who writes music

masterpieces works of outstanding skill

mazurka a lively Polish folk dance

romantic an era of music popular between 1820 and 1900

salons places where people gathered to hear music and exchange ideas

tuberculosis a disease that affects the lungs

tutor a private teacher

variation music that includes changes to an original piece of music, much like the remixes of modern music today.

Read More About Chopin

Venezia, Mike. *Frederic Chopin*. Children's Press, 2017.

Weill, Catherine. *Fryderyk Chopin*. First Discovery Music, 2017.

Whiting, Jim. *The Life and Times of Frederic Chopin*. Mitchell Lane Publishers, 2004.

Index

Bach, Johann Sebastian 9
Chopin, Nicholas 6
Dudevant, Aurore 24
Elsner, Jozef 12
Mozart, Wolfgang 9
Paris 14, 22, 24, 27, 29
Poland, Warsaw 6, 31
Sand, George 24
Vienna 14, 17–18, 22
Zywny, Wojciech 9